I0763009

American Commerce & American Union.

REVIEW,

BY

SAMUEL B. RUGGLES,

OF THE ADDRESS OF THE

HON. MR. BANKS,

AT THE MERCHANTS' EXCHANGE, NEW YORK,

WITH THE

REPLY AND REJOINDER.

NEW YORK:
D. APPLETON & CO.,
346 AND 348 BROADWAY.
1856.

Hall, Clayton & Co., Printers,
46 Pine Street, N. Y.

A REVIEW OF THE ADDRESS

DELIVERED AT THE MERCHANTS' EXCHANGE, BY THE

Hon. Mr. BANKS,

Speaker of the House of Representatives of the United States.

This "Review,"—with the exception of the note at page 14, on the pecuniary value of Southern trade to Northern cities,—originally appeared in *The New York Commercial Advertiser*. It was written in compliance with the request contained in the following letter:

SAMUEL B. RUGGLES, ESQ., NEW YORK, *Sept.* 30, 1856.

DEAR SIR—We respectfully ask you to give some attention to the address delivered by Mr. Banks, of Massachusetts, on Thursday last, on the steps of the Merchants' Exchange, in this city. We think it contains fallacies which ought to be exposed, and the task of their exposure cannot be entrusted to any gentleman better qualified, from your long and intimate official connection* with the internal and external commerce of the country, to comprehend and review the great commercial theme to which Mr. Banks professedly addressed himself. If you can comply with this request, you will greatly serve the cause of legitimate commerce, and gratify a number of merchants and other citizens, among whom are

Your friends and fellow citizens,

HIRAM KETCHUM,
CH. AUG. DAVIS,
A. C. KINGSLAND,
WILLIAM B. ASTOR,
SHEPHERD KNAPP,
THEODORE DEHON,
HOWELL L. WILLIAMS,
WILLIAM CHAUNCEY,
CHESTER DRIGGS, and others.

---

* Mr. Ruggles was Chairman of the Committee of Ways and Means of the New York Assembly in 1838, and for several years afterwards President of the Board of Canal Commissioners of the State.

To this letter Mr. RUGGLES returned the following answer:

GENTLEMEN:—Permit me to express my thanks for the kind and respectful terms in which you have seen fit to call my attention to the address recently delivered at the Merchants' Exchange, of this city, by the Hon. Mr. BANKS, Speaker of the House of Representatives of the United States. Under the circumstances, I cannot withhold the opinion you request me to express. The coming election, the most important since the formation of the Government, involving in its possible, if not its probable consequences the future destiny of the American Republic and the American Continent, is necessarily a matter of the deepest and most vital interest to all whose lot, like ours, is cast in this its commercial capital and centre. We have all of us labored as best we could to build up its present prosperity, and secure its honorable renown, and none of us can now remain indifferent to an event which may seriously check its onward career, if it do not lead to its utter prostration and ruin.

The great struggle now agitating the American Union has called forth the address in question—from one occupying nearly the highest office in the Government. In this address the Speaker of the National House of Representatives, standing in the commercial heart of the nation, maintains as a cardinal political truth that the executive power of the Union ought permanently to be committed to the Northern States. Not that a proposition so bold is uttered in express terms, but the whole philosophy of his address rests upon it.

To maintain this dogma, the Speaker exhibits before the men of business of New York an array of statistics from which he deduces his political conclusions. It is due to the address to admit that its language, with some exceptions, is dignified, and at times animated and impressive. It bears marks of elaborate preparation, and is well calculated to mislead an unthinking and unexamining multitude. Its admirers, who control the Republican press, declare it to be most eloquent, comprehensive and statesmanlike; and, from its rapid circulation through the Union, it is evidently intended as the great intellectual effort of the campaign. As a citizen of New York, to be affected by its doctrines, I therefore yield to your invitation to examine somewhat the accuracy of its statements, and, if time shall permit, the soundness of its conclusions.

The fundamental proposition and cardinal idea of the address is that the sixteen non-slaveholding States greatly exceed and excel the remaining fifteen slaveholding States in all the legitimate pursuits of national industry, and that this is proved by comparing their respective products of material wealth; and upon this allegation the Speaker contends that the sixteen non-slaveholding States are now entitled to direct the government of the Union.

The reason assigned for this alleged superiority is the existence of slavery in the fifteen States, a region where, in Mr. Banks' language, "there is one man down and another man holding him down, one portion of the people *doing nothing* and another portion of the same people helping them to do nothing." This is his first reason; and the second, which he denominates "*the secret* that accounts for the difference," is that the men of the South *abandoning agriculture* for the time, and having no literature, no science, no inventive power, no mechanical or manufacturing industry, "have given their whole attention to the government of the country." "They are *immersed*," says Mr. Banks, "in the methods of obtaining offices of honor, of emolument and trust from the Federal Government."

Having thus philosophically discovered the secret of the evil, Mr. Banks' remedy is obvious. It is to deprive these misguided men of their offices; for, says he, "What will they do, when they are DESPOILED of their offices of honor and trust and emolument in the ARMY and NAVY, and the Federal Government?" "I will tell you," adds he, "what they will do. They are out of the government, according to their own statement. They must do something, and that necessity will turn them immediately to the increase of the material wealth of that section of the country." "They will come North!" "They will go into the middle of the States," and there they will "see men operating with mechanical inventions"—"and what," asks he, "will the Southern men then do, but provide a *substitute for slave labor*, by the adoption of the mechanical inventions that have distinguished the industry of the Eastern Middle States?" "Thus," says he, "by this single change, we will pave the way *for a vast change* in the history and the institutions of this Government."

Here, then, is the successful solution of the great political and economical problem, which heretofore has tasked the highest wisdom of our patriots and philanthropists. The proper distribution of the black race over the American continent—the grand continental result supposed by some short-sighted statesmen to be a work for generations, if not centuries yet to come—is to be attained in November next, simply by "despoiling the South of their offices in the Army, the Navy, and the Federal Government."

Now, when we consider that not more than 50,000, at the utmost, of the total Southern white population of seven millions, are in possession of the offices in question,—and that it is not certain that all even of them will undertake, after their ejection, the task of wandering through the North to examine the mechanical contrivances for dispensing with slave labor—it may be doubted whether the means provided by the statesmanship of Mr. Banks will prove quite adequate to the end. It is gratifying, however, to learn from him that he does not regard this general sweep of his "Southern brethren" from the army and navy as a sectional process, but views it as an eminently fraternal and national proceeding. "With the institutions of the Southern States," says he, "local or traditional, we have nothing to do," and "I dismiss the matter by asserting that the declaration that we intend to interfere in their affairs is a bold and baseless slander." Contenting himself simply with turning them out of office, because they are slaveholders, and with their consequent efforts to substitute mechanical inventions for slave labor, he refrains from inquiring what is to become of the four millions of helpless blacks whose labor is thus superseded.

He deems it quite a subordinate matter to inquire whether these four millions of blacks, who in thirty years will increase to ten millions, are to be sent further South, and where—or distributed among the States, and which,—or sent to the Amazon, or to the Niger,—or left to perish by starvation, or to cut their own throats or their masters'. Details so petty, the comprehensive statesmanship of Mr. Banks does not condescend to embrace.

And now for the statistics of the address which drew down the enthusiastic plaudits of the intelligent audience assembled in Wall Street. They are certainly very remarkable, dealing with matters in no small way, but presenting pictures that inflame the imagination with the sublimest visions of national glory.

Mr. Banks himself is profoundly convinced, not only of their importance, but of their accuracy. Hear him: "In what I have to say to you I mean to rely upon GREAT FACTS, ABOVE *all question as to their truth;* and facts which, if admitted, *remove all questions* as to the policy by which we should be directed in the impending controversy between twenty-seven millions of freemen for the chief offices of the republic." "I see before me a nation which has produced results such as the world never before has witnessed, and such as the mind of no intelligent man *has heretofore* been able to conceive," and then comes the GREAT FACT—embodying a proposition so vast and comprehensive, and yet so condensed, that the orator declares it to be "the product of all that he has to say." In its grand simplicity it is this, that the people of the United States in the year 1856 "will give to the world as their portion of the industrial product of the human race *forty-five hundred millions of dollars!*" "a sum greater by an eighth than the entire national debt of the British Empire that has been accumulating for two centuries."

The newspapers inform us that the annunciation of this result was received with loud applause by the crowd in Wall Street. How far that commendation was creditable to the intelligence of those who bestowed it, let us briefly examine.

In the first place, if it were true that the nation produces forty-five hundred millions annually, it does not "remove all questions in the impending controversy" whether we shall elect Mr. Fremont to the Presidency and "despoil our Southern brethren of their offices in the army and navy." If the North produced the whole forty-five hundred millions, and the South did nothing whatever but keep the black race in subjection, it would not follow that the South should be excluded from all participation in the Government; for if, as some contend, the black race be nothing but a burthen on the community which contains it, the freemen of the North should be thankful to the South for bearing the whole of the burthen, and thus leaving them unfettered to accumulate that forty-five hundred millions annually.

But, unhappily for Mr. Banks and his admiring auditors, it is not true that the nation annually produces the 4500 millions—for look at his own analysis. Fifteen hundred millions, says he, are produced by manufacturing and mechanical industry; sixteen hundred by agriculture. This makes thirty-one; and the residue, 1400 millions, where does it come from? Let the commingled rhetoric and statistics of Mr. Banks answer: "THE SEAS, that are whitened with the flags of the commerce of New York, each signalizing the name, the character, the affluence, the business, the influence of its merchant princes, *contribute to this great product* of 4500 millions —*fourteen hundred millions* as the share of commerce."

Now, gentlemen, what do the seas thus rhetorically whitened, in fact, produce? That is to say; what articles of commercial value? They produce a good many codfish, many mackerel, and here and there a whale; the total value whereof, when caught, barrelled and landed in the United States, hardly exceeds twenty millions annually, if it amounts to that. The portion of those products exported in the year 1855 was less than four millions. The remainder, then, of Mr. Banks' imaginary fourteen hundred millions consists wholly of the very products of agricultural, manufacturing, and mechanical industry which commerce had placed on the seas, but which had been previously computed and embraced in his first two items of fifteen and sixteen hundred millions. And thus we behold the Speaker, in his very first plunge into the sea of figures, going astray to the tune of *thirteen hundred and ninety-six millions*. If this be the "music of the Union" which Mr. Banks describes the Northern ploughboy as whistling, his political psalmody, to say the least, is capable of improvement.

But again: The Speaker asserts that of the 1600 millions produced by agriculture, the fifteen slave states contribute but 45 per cent. How this assertion is proved does not appear, but if it be true it does not show the slave states to fall short of their just proportion, for they have less than forty per cent. of the total population, and only thirty per cent. of the white population. Why, then, should their agriculture be required to produce even forty-five per cent.?

But the truth of the statement must be more than doubtful. The very sun of the South, so unfavorable to white labor as to make a black population necessary, is peculiarly favorable to agricultural development. Time is wanting to compute the comparative product even of cereals—but if flocks and herds form part of a nation's wealth, and mankind has held them to be things of value since the days of Abraham, then the South in this important element very far exceeds the North. The census shows nine millions of cattle standing South of the Potomac belonging to seven millions of white men, and only eight millions North of it, belonging to fourteen millions of whites; and what statesman, entitled for an instant to the epithet, does not perceive the rapid increase of the cotton crop? It may be true, as the Speaker ventures to assert, that the men of the South abandon agriculture in quest of office, but the official statistical tables do not show it.

But again: Mr. Banks was addressing and affecting to instruct a body of merchants—a commercial community from the steps of their own Exchange. Why, on such an occasion and with such an audience, did he omit to state the respective proportions which the agriculture of the South and of the North contributed to the commerce that whitened the seas? Did he not know that of the 1600 millions produced by agriculture, at least 1200 millions are consumed on the spot, and never reach the sea at all? For how much of the hundreds of millions estimated as the value of the hay, and cattle, and poultry, and milk, and eggs, which help to swell the aggregate, is carried at all in the vessels of the merchant princes? How much even of the three hundred millions of Indian corn goes to sea?

And above all, does not Mr. Banks know, and do not the New York merchants know, that of every 100 millions of Southern cotton, at least 90 go to sea; and 14 out of every 20 millions of Southern tobacco? While of the total product of Northern agriculture, estimated by Mr. Banks at 880 millions, less than 40 millions are exported either to foreign countries or coastwise?

Does he not see, and do not all of us, whether merchant, banker, landowner, or mechanic, see and feel that the agriculture of the South thus disparaged furnishes the very foundation of our commercial prosperity? And can this great trading, navigating city be induced, by any pompous and idle parade of imaginary thousands of millions, to dissolve their fraternal and national connection with the whole magnificent domain spread out South of the Potomac—the very *Indies* of the American Republic—and aid Mr. Banks and his associates in excluding that grand division of the Union from all participation in the honors and emoluments of the government?

But I find the subject growing on my hands, beyond the limits of a single letter, and I must reserve for a further communication the remarks on Mr Banks's political deductions and his statistics of foreign commerce, which the subject requires.

NEW YORK, 2d October, 1856.

To Messrs. HIRAM KETCHUM, C. A. DAVIS, A. C. KINGSLAND, WM. B. ASTOR, SHEPHERD KNAPP, and others.

GENTLEMEN:—I closed my letter of yesterday, after attempting to vindicate the material industry of the Southern portion of the American Union from the disparaging comparison made at the Merchants' Exchange, in the address of Mr. Banks, the Speaker of the House of Representatives of the United States.

In view of the peculiar geographical importance of that section of our common country, and the character and value of its products, I ventured to call it "the *Indies* of the American Republic." The phrase was not selected for any merely rhetorical purpose, but simply as a term of description, affording the means of arithmetical comparison.

A moment's examination of the history of Europe will show that nearly all its civilized nations have sought to increase their commercial and political power, by acquiring territories or colonies enjoying a tropical climate and yielding tropical products. But these dependencies have always been widely separated from the parent state. The West Indies of England, of Spain, of France, and of Holland lie far away, across a stormy ocean—while the East Indies of the same powers are separated by the breadth of a hemisphere.

But the Indies of the American Republic lie within its very borders, and are bounded by the Chesapeake and the Gulf of Mexico.

They are cheaply and constantly accessible by the commercial and navigating states, both by land and by water—not only by the open ocean in front, but by the great national navigable river of the interior, flowing uninterruptedly from the land of the oak and the pine to that of the palm and the olive. And herein lies the deep secret, the very inner life of our national existence—furnishing the key to our commercial and political history for ages to come.

How singular, then, the spectacle of a statesman disparaging this geographical portion of our wide-spread empire, for the reason merely that its pursuits are mainly agricultural, while those of his immediate neighbors are mechanical and manufacturing. Does he not see, and can he not feel, that this very difference of pursuit, growing out of difference of climate, is a providential boon, bestowed upon our nation for the very purpose of creating the necessity for national commerce and national communion? Does he not perceive that if the cotton planters of the Carolinas made pins and buttons and wooden clocks, they would not buy the pins and buttons and wooden clocks of New England? That if the cotton plant grew on the shores of Massachusetts, the cotton planters would not be shod by the shoemakers of Lynn? Can he not understand the great truth that the nation's difference is only the nation's peace? that New York and Pennsylvania are geographically interposed, as commercial agents, to bind in harmony by the golden bonds of commerce these remote extremities, discordant only in name, and harmonious in their mutual interests and necessities?

But let us look a little at the arithmetic of the case. Let us ascertain the pecuniary value of the geographical conjunction in a single nation, on a single, unbroken continent of the temperate and the tropical regions—and for this purpose, let us compare the East Indies of the British Empire with the Indies forming an integral, continental portion of the American Republic.

The British territories in India, including the tributary states under their authority, embrace 1,200,000 square miles and 140 millions of people. Their total commerce with England in the year 1832 amounted only to ten millions and eighty-seven thousand pounds sterling—a little less than fifty millions of dollars. In the same year the products of our American Indies, between the Chesapeake and the Gulf, directly exported to foreign countries, were 42 millions of dollars; and the residue sent to the North, either for export or consumption, were certainly not less than twenty millions—being in all 62 millions. This sum was returned to the South in equivalent imports, making a total trade of 124 millions—more than double of that of British India.

In the 20 years that have since elapsed, these two great commercial empires of the world have been running an animated race—for under the vigorous and enlightened administration of the elder England, its annual commerce with British India has swollen from the ten millions sterling to twenty-six millions five hundred and fifty thousand pounds, or one hundred and thirty millions of dollars, while the energy of this new England of the Western

World has enlarged the trade of its American Indies from 124 to nearly 350 millions of dollars.

I am unfortunate in not possessing Mr. Banks's happy faculty for dealing with millions by the thousand, and must fain content myself with creeping along by hundreds of millions—but I will aver that these our Southern States, which he deems it proper and patriotic to disparage, do now actually and annually contribute at least 300 millions to the commercial strength of the Republic; and I will further predict, that if the American Union can be preserved from the assaults of demagogues and sentimentalists and half-crazed fanatics, this same 300 millions before the close of the present century will nearly approach, if it do not entirely reach, one thousand millions—animating and invigorating to a corresponding extent every department of national and continental industry, and every element of national and continental strength.

The question is then presented to the merchants, mechanics and landowners of this great continental metropolis—to the million of inhabitants congregated around the bay of New York, already possessing a thousand millions of wealth, the very product of the Union—itself the very type and exponent of the Union—do they approve the political proposition to despoil the South of every national office, and deprive it of all participation in the government of the Union?

If we look further into the address of Mr. Banks, we shall find ourselves comforted by the assurance that other regions remain on the globe far more valuable to us than the Southern States. "We propose," says he, "if the people of the *North* should conceive and *inaugurate a policy of their own,*" among other things, "to cultivate amicable relations" with neighboring nations, and especially with the South American continent. "For look!" says Mr. Banks, "at the South American States. What do we see in South America? A territory *ten times* as large as that of the United States—a country more fertile than *any portion* of the United States. While we give 4,500 millions annually of accumulated industry, South America is capable of giving four, *ten*—nay, even ONE HUNDRED times more of accumulated industry. She has twenty millions of population and ten millions of square miles."*

* How far do these "GREAT FACTS, *above all question as to their truth,*" agree with the reality?

South America has but 6,310,000 square miles, and the United States 2,936,000, or

Now let us coolly count these sums:—Four times 4,500 millions are 18,000 millions; ten times 4,500 millions are 45,000 millions; one hundred times 4,500 millions are 450,000 millions, or written out arithmetically in a single line, $450,000,000,000. Oh! Mr. Banks! why did you leave your own sensible and sober State of Massachusetts to come among us poor barbarians, to dazzle our eyes and turn our brains with this effulgent row of figures? But savages are caught by glitter and gew-gaw. Let them swallow the 450,000 millions and be thankful.

But even here the "eloquent and comprehensive" speaker does not stop. Even the 450,000 millions fail to satisfy his imperial appetite. The two continents of America did tolerably for a beginning. But a richer repast must be added, drawn from the long-buried stores of the dead, old oriental world, where the statesman sees a still more glorious vision. "Look," says he, "at where we stand! Here is Wall Street! On the spot to which we now direct our eyes, we are twenty days' journey from the populous cities of Hindostan, of China, *and* of Asia,—the depositories *of the world's wealth* for hundreds, and for thousands, and for *tens of thousands* of years—a wealth which is fabulous in its origin, fabulous in its extent, and is the accumulated wealth of seven hundred millions of people."

Now, gentlemen, I am getting almost tired of "accumulated wealth;" but as Mr. Banks proposes that we make a railway to the Pacific, to reach this accumulation of tens of thousands of years, I will merely observe first, that it has probably grown somewhat musty by this time—and next, that I fear Mr. Warren Hastings and his worthy successors have got ahead of us; inasmuch as the total

---

nearly *one half*. The total population of South America, embracing all races and colors, the result of three centuries of civilization, does not exceed 18 millions. Many portions of the United States, especially of the South, if not more fertile, are far more commercially productive than large portions of South America. Georgia and Alabama may surely challenge comparison with Patagonia and the Pampas.

In the year 1853 the total exports to the United States of the whole continent from Panama to Cape Horn, amounted only to $22,875,183. In the same year the exports to foreign countries of Cotton and other products of the Southern States of the American Union, and not including the large amounts sent to the Northern States for consumption, were 124 millions, and in the 11 years from 1844 to 1855, *nine hundred and eighty-six* millions.

The freights and commissions on that enormous sum, and a like equivalent amount returned in imports, and mainly earned by Northern vessels and Northern merchants, will sufficiently account for the growth of Northern commercial cities.

The annual commerce of the City of New York through the Hudson River and the Erie Canal is about 200 millions of dollars. The Southern trade through the Atlantic falls little short of that amount, and its loss would inevitably depopulate one fourth, if not one third of the city.—S. B. R.

commerce of this same Hindostan amounted in the year 1832 to less than fifty millions, as is above shown.

But seriously. No man who loves the Union will object to a railway to the Pacific, nor even to two railways, one from the Northern and the other from the Southern States. They are works of urgent continental necessity, not for the purpose so absurdly proclaimed of gathering up the accumulated wealth of tens of thousands of years, as for the plain practical object of preserving the integrity of our great continental Union, and preventing its Pacific division from being dismembered from the Atlantic.

But does Mr. Banks or any of his admirers imagine that under the administration of Mr. Fremont, and the violent agitation if not positive disruption that must inevitably ensue, the country will be in any humor or any condition to prosecute these vast and difficult undertakings, requiring peace and repose, and the cordial acquiescence and patriotic union of all parties, with a wise, upright and conciliatory President at the head? "California," says Mr. Banks, "is the child of the compromise of 1850." And if so, who so likely to preserve it to the Union as he who brought it in? To whom can the task be more properly committed than to MILLARD FILLMORE, the well-tried statesman, whose name is stamped with imperishable honor on that very compromise?

Under his wise and beneficent administration, the country would again return to the peace in which he left it. Common sense and common justice would resume their accustomed sway. Our merchants might not be favored with exciting addresses, disparaging their Southern brethren, and sowing the seeds of fratricidal strife, but they would enjoy the tranquil blessings of a paternal and impartial government, protecting the interests, and respecting not only the rights, but the feelings of all who claim as their common heritage that august and glorious Union, which God has graciously entrusted to our keeping, to test and to try our justice, our forecast, our forbearance, and our wisdom.

With cordial regard,

I remain, faithfully, your friend,

SAMUEL B. RUGGLES,

24 Union Square, N.Y.

Mr. BANKS to Mr. RUGGLES.

REPLY.

First published October 24, 1856.

Chicago, *October* 14, 1856.

Samuel B. Ruggles, Esq.:

Sir—Until I reached this city, I had not an opportunity to examine your letters of the 30th September and the 2nd October, or the speeches of the gentlemen who have given their comments to the public upon my address in Wall Street on the 25th of last month. Constant engagements in different and distant States have compelled my absence, and will account for my delay in making the following suggestions upon one of the topics of your letters. They relate to the industrial interests of the country, and are in no respect of a partisan character.

To Governor Floyd's argument I have nothing to say. The only point I notice is one in which he misrepresents one of the positions of my speech, and makes a misstatement of fact—depreciating the strength of his own part of the country in the element of population, which is the second element of prosperity in every State, for the purpose of strengthening an erroneous deduction from his own misstatement. I stated that of twenty-seven millions of people in the United States in 1855, the South had ten millions. Gov. Floyd assumes that the South has but eight millions, and thus, with less than half the population, produces *per capita* more than its share of our industrial product. Upon a reference to the financial reports of last year, Gov. Floyd will find that the *per capita* product is about $65.67 for each person in the Southern States, to $106 in the North.

Gov. Hunt finds great pleasure, it appears, in the fact that the "statistical computation, which presented results almost fabulous of American industry," has been reduced about fourteen or fifteen (hundred) "millions of dollars by the clear investigation of one of the ablest statesmen of New York." This reduction which affords the Governor so great a pleasure, and which he thinks does New York so much honor, relates exclusively to commercial industry.

It is not asserted that the agricultural or manufacturing industry is over-estimated. Your effort at reduction relates only to the sum over $3,100,000,000 which constitutes the balance of $4,500.000,000, stated as the aggregate of American industry, and of which $1,200,000,000 was credited to commerce, and the satisfaction of Governor Hunt is derived from your assumed success. There are people, who, doing nothing themselves, believe that nothing is done—who think the highest honor that can be conferred upon any class is the privilege of doing nothing. Associating with industry only the ideas of perspiration and fatigue, they hail with joy any successful attempt to show that the amount of labor has been overrated. One would have supposed that in New York commercial industry would have made an exception in this philosophy. You, sir, speaking for the merchants would have it otherwise; but you are mistaken. I have neither over-estimated the detailed, nor aggregated industry of our people. On the contrary, I have *greatly under-estimated each and all*, and *especially I fear, that which relates to commerce.* Nor did I anticipate that my desire to properly present our gigantic commercial movements would be assailed in New York as my chief error, by one especially claiming to represent its mercantile interests.

Before I re-state the industrial facts, and the authority upon which they stand, which I repeat "are great facts, beyond all question" as to their truth, I beg your permission to say, that at the outset you mistake an illustration for a proposition. You say, "the fundamental and cardinal idea of the address is, that sixteen non-slaveholding States greatly exceed and excel the remaining fifteen slaveholding States in all the legitimate pursuits of national industry," &c. Pardon me, sir; the fundamental idea of my address, on the contrary, was that the government had been surrendered to the propagation of abstract ideas, and of institutions at war with all successful national industry, and that it was now time that it should be turned, for a little while at least, to the development of the material interests of the continent. We asked for peace and a wider field of industry. The industrial facts to which you refer, and the bloody history of Kansas to which you make no allusion, were cited as illustrations of the proposition. Nor did I claim, as you say, "that the Northern States are now entitled to direct the government." My assertion was, that those who had so great a share in the labor of developing the material wealth of the continent, should also have a part in shaping its political policy. We invited all to join us who would substitute industrial and commercial development for sectional agitation and pro-slavery propagandism. Those only denounce it as sectional who make it so.

But you say, "unhappily for Mr. Banks, it is not true that the nation annually produces $4,500,000,000." Happily for Mr. Ruggles, it may be true. Let us see. My statement was, that of this aggregate industry agriculture contributed $1,600,000,000; manufacturing and mechanical industry, $1,500,000,000; and that commerce gave us $1,200,000,000, leaving a balance of $200,000,000 as the product of the forest, fisheries and mines, to which I did not allude in my speech. Now, sir, for the first product, I give you as my authority the census returns of 1840 and 1850. The product of agricultural industry for 1840 was $564,772,785. That of 1850 was $956,924,640. Allowing only the same ratio of increase for the six years since 1850 as for the ten years from 1840 to 1850, and the product is nearly the sum I stated. But the increase is much greater. The extent of land cultivated and the quantity of seed sown has been increased beyond that of any former period, and the now universal use of agricultural improvements, with the rapid increase of population, will give us a far more rapid increase of agricultural industry. Mr. Andrews, in his report upon the salt trade, estimates the product of agriculture for 1852 at $1,700,000,000. Mr. De Bow estimates the product of 1854 at $1,600,000,000. The industrial product of Massachusetts alone, as shown by the census of 1855, had risen from the sum of $124,735,000 in 1850, to $300,000,000 in 1855. My estimate of the product of agricultural industry may very well stand, therefore, upon this basis. As to manufacturing and mechanical industry, I give the same authority. By the census of 1840 it was $441,360,814. In 1850 it was $1,055,594,899—an increase of more than 100 per cent. With the same ratio of increase for the past six years, the product will exceed my estimate; and you will readily see, for reasons that need not here be stated, that the ratio of increase will be much greater for the present than for the last decimal period, and this does not include the yearly increase of dwellings, churches and shops. I think, therefore, the estimate for this branch of American industry will stand your investigation.

Now, as to commerce. I came to New York, as the seat of commercial industry, to speak of commerce. You have investigated the product of the fisheries. I did not allude to that subject. Had I desired to speak of the fisheries I would have gone to Marblehead, or possibly to St. Johns. I did not suppose that in New York it would be necessary to define the meaning of the term commerce, which I understand to be the exchange of product for product; and permit me to say, that it is a *branch of industry that greatly exceeds even my estimate.* Allow me, sir, to state the basis upon which that estimate was made.

American commerce embraces the transmission and exchange of products for products, upon canal, river, lake, sea and ocean. It includes the railway, so far as it is used for commercial purposes. Let us look, then, at the capital invested in these engines of commerce. There are 5,212,000 tons shipping, which valued at $75 per ton, is $390,900,000. There were in operation in 1854, according to De Bow's census compendium, 4,798 miles of canal, costing, at $24,000 per mile, $115,000,000. There were in use, December, 1855, 21,440 miles of railway, costing, at an outlay of $30,000 per miles for construction and equipment, $643,000,000, and in which, according to Mr. Hunt's estimate, there is invested a capital of $700,000,000. Here is an aggregate capital of $1,205,000,000 invested in enterprises that are exclusively commercial, except only in the transport of passengers. I think the merchants of New York may regard this investment as deserving consideration.

Let us consider the business transacted upon these commercial lines. I give upon this subject as the best authority, the report of J. D. Andrews, Esq., Consul General to the Canadas, upon the colonial and lake commerce. He estimates the annual average freight business of our railways as equal to 1,000 tons per mile. He states that on several long routes it is equal to 2,000 tons per mile. So far as I have been able to obtain information, upon inquiry, of the freight of western railroads, it exceeds 1,000 tons per mile. Excluding iron and coal, the freight is estimated at $100 per ton, and the aggregate freight thus annually transported over 21,440 miles of railroad is equal to 21,440,000 tons, and valued at an average of $100 per ton, according to his estimate, it is equal to $2,144,000,000.

Now as to canal commerce, assuming upon the same authority

that the average yearly freight transmitted by canals is 6,000 tons per mile, the aggregate freight for one year will be equal to 28,968,000 tons for the 4,798 miles of canal, and this valued at $66 per ton, is equal to freight value of $1,951,888,000. The estimate per mile is based upon the returns of the New York canals for 1851, which was equal to 9,000 tons per mile.

From the report of the Secretary of the Treasury, for 1855, it appears that the tonnage employed in the coasting trade was equal to 2,498,108 tons. Allowing upon the authority before cited, 20,000 gross tons for each ton of shipping, as its trade for one year, the aggregate is 60,000,000 tons, which at a mean value of $81.60 per ton amounts to $4,881,000.

The officially reported value of the foreign commerce in 1855 is $536,624,366. Let me recapitulate these results:

	Tons.	*Value.*
Railway commerce........	21,440,000	$2,144,000,000
Canal do.	28,968,000	1,951,888,000
Coastwise do.	60,000,000	4,881,000,000
Foreign do.	—	536,624,366
Total		$9,513,512,366

This aggregate embraces so much of the product of agricultural and manufacturing industry as enters into commerce, whether it be more or less. It also includes the re-sale and re-shipment of the same article as often as it shall occur; and it includes as well the increased value that is given by commerce to industrial products of whatever character, which is very great.

We have, then, a capital of $1,205,000,000, which deducting so much as will be equal to the expense of the transportation of passengers, is used exclusively in the domestic and foreign commerce of the American people, transporting by railway, canal, river, lake, sea, and ocean, commercial values equal to the sum of $9,513,-512,366.

The interest and earnings of this capital—the compensation of nearly seven hundred thousand of the most active, enterprising and intelligent men of this continent, and the increased value given to products by transportation and re-transportation, by sale and re-sale, by aggregation and by division—is the product of commercial industry. It is neither agricultural nor mechanical product. Will you inform us what that amount is? Is it five per cent.? Is it twenty-five per cent.? I have ventured to estimate it at less than twelve per centum; and this gives the sum I have stated as the aggregate of our commercial industry. It may be said that the detailed estimates are extravagant. Well, sir, reduce them; deduct a fifth; subtract a fourth; diminish the gross estimates one half, and still it will sustain my conclusion. The merchants of New York will, of course, admit that something has been accomplished. Mr. Secretary Walker estimated the industrial product of 1846 at $3,000,000,000. Nearly one-third of the sum must have been derived from the labor of those engaged in the exchange of product for product, for the agricultural and manufacturing industry of 1846 could not have exceeded that of 1850, as shown by the census. Since that year we have added to the territory of the United States 523,000 square miles; we have added to the coast shore line 3,695 miles, being more than a tenth part of our entire shore line—always an important element in the commercial prosperity of nations; to our population we have added more than six millions; and to our industrial product all that which springs from mechanical improvements and increased mental and physical vigor. If it were $3,000,000,000 in 1846, it certainly is not over-estimated at $4,500,000,000 in 1856. It may be said that this is but a mere approximation to the truth. I grant it, but it is approximations only that are attainable. Statistical information has been hitherto under the ban of our government. It is recently only that detailed information has been sought, and our census returns have been discredited because they were imperfect. The statistics of manufactures, gathered by the government in 1850, have not yet been printed.

I do not undervalue territorial acquisitions, but I have no hesitation in saying that perfect "knowledge of our industry and our capacity for industrial results would be more valuable to us than the annexation of the Mexican States to the republic. Statistical information is to a people what the log is to the navigator, or the balance sheet to the merchant. The unexampled growth of Western cities is as much owing to the constant and minute publication of the facts attending their advance as to any other cause. Out of the rich treasures of accurate and complete statistical returns we could draw conclusions far more surprising than that which has startled you, and deduce a philosophy as full of instruction and beauty as any which springs from a contemplation of the ideal or physical world.

You were pleased to remark upon the facility with which the results of our industry was stated in millions and thousands of millions. I desired only to present an adequate idea of the industry of thirty millions of people in figures, which always stand for limited quantities. If you prefer it, I will give you, as a substitute for my figures, the sober and staid words of Mr. Calhoun, who said that a conception of the probable commercial industry of the Mississippi valley, not of the Union, " was beyond the power of any man's imagination."

You are pleased also to contrast, in depreciating terms, the commerce of the Indies with that of the Southern States. It is not the first time that the commerce of the East has been thus discredited. When the English merchants were endeavoring to enlarge their commercial relations with the East, it was invariably declared that the trade of the Indies could not be increased. You, too, also measure the future by the present, and overlooking the elements of power which constitute a capacity for commerce—land, population and capital—assume that the Southern States have a commercial future equal to that possessed by seven hundred millions of people, with the accumulated capital of centuries, and a limitless territory, of which any one State could supply the world with every variety of tropical wealth. Extent of commerce is not measured by existing trade merely, but by possible capacity for product and exchange. You might as well declare a guano island worthless because it had no value when discovered.

But " the South," you say, " is the very Indies;" in what regard, sir? We are told that the Indies are distinguished by a combination of caste, that the people are separated into classes, of which only the upper class is allowed to receive or impart information; that private or public wrongs are avenged by assassins, who constitute an "order" in the State. Pray, sir, what constitutes the South, "the very Indies?" and who are the Thugs of this newly discovered seat of wealth?

No, sir, the Indies of the Western hemisphere are not the Southern States. They will ultimately be found rather in the Southern Continent. It is not, however, in the West, alone, that we should look for limits to our commercial enterprise. No pent up seas should restrain us. Throughout the Globe, East and West, North and South, we should seek that accumulation of wealth which rewards enlightened commerce, and gives, in the language of Sir Walter Raleigh, "with the world's wealth, the conquest of the world."

Allow me, sir, in conclusion, one word of apology. My speech was made under circumstances of much embarrassment. I had been suddenly summoned, by telegraph, to attend the meeting several days earlier than the day first appointed. So far as its language was concerned, it was delivered without the premeditation of a single moment. Within twelve hours from the time when the last word was spoken it was in print, ready for distribution through the mails. The report was without the revision or knowledge of the speaker, and the reporter could, by no possibility, have anticipated an idea or topic of the speech. An address of two hours, reported and published with remarkable accuracy under such circumstances and in so brief a time, would have suggested to any one not utterly buried in the past, a possibility at least, that other remarkable industrial results might have been produced. You failed to appreciate either; but I trust that the merchants of your city, making due allowance for a word or sentence misreported or misspoken, will readily admit that equally important advances may have been made in other industrial pursuits

Since the days of Consul Planchus,
When George the First was Young.

With fitting acknowledgments to those who, by inviting your criticisms, have afforded me an opportunity of explanation and reply,

I am very truly, your fellow-citizen, &c.,

N. P. BANKS, Jr.

Mr. RUGGLES to Speaker BANKS.

REJOINDER.

New York, *October* 30*th*, 1856.

To the Honorable Nathaniel P. Banks, Jr.,
Speaker of the House of Representatives of the United States:

Sir: On the 25th of September last you honored our city with a public address, delivered at the Merchants' Exchange, in which you pointed out what you deemed to be the sources of its prosperity, present and prospective. As a matter of course, "the character, the affluence, the business and influence of our merchant princes,"—our "magnificent streets,"—our "magnificent bays and noble rivers,"—our "naval structures, from the little tender to the magnificent steamer, that has astonished the world with its prowess,"—were all brought forward and eulogized in the terms customary on such occasions. In addition to these familiar phrases, the riches of a commerce yet to be opened "by well-directed and intelligent industry," with Cuba,—with South America,—with Central America,—with Hindostan and China and Western Asia, were held up to our delighted eyes. Coming down to particulars, you assured us that within ten years we should control the iron market of the world, and might increase our trade 200 per cent., "and in regard to cotton more than that." Can you wonder that your auditors united with loud acclamations, in pronouncing your address a splendid performance?

It so happened that some of our steady citizens, whose lives had been particularly devoted to the business of constructing the internal communications leading to the metropolis, on scrutinizing your statements, discovered a tone of disparagement, if not of injustice, toward the Southern portion of the American Union—a region which they regarded as contributing largely and vitally to the prosperity of the city; and they found, moreover, a vein of excessive exaggeration in respect to the commercial power and industry of the North, which they thought repugnant to good sense and proper national feeling.

With every sentiment of respect for the high office you occupy, and without any personal unkindness toward yourself, I nevertheless participated in these opinions, and in two letters published on the 1st of October, and the day preceding, I gave my reasons. For taking this liberty, the Republican press has denominated me "a *fossil*," and some go to the length of ranking me among "the *high fossils*." I cannot well except to that stony epithet, feeling that my opinion of your address remains and must remain fixed as flint.

I still believe, and ever shall believe, that its tendency was and is to aggravate the feeling of disunion and disloyalty already too rife,—and that its statements and deductions were and are alike erroneous and mischievous. My criticism of its statistics has now drawn from you the letter of the 14th, published in the *Herald* of the 24th and the *Courier* of the 25th instant. The latter of these journals, in its leading article of the 8th, had declared that the "sensation" produced by your address "was deep and permanent," —that "it yet endures and is exercising a great influence upon the progress of the campaign." But it was pleased to add, that "little people could not be quiet," but "must needs quibble and cavil at your statistics."

Commencing your letter of the 14th in a similar tone, you indulge in a fling at "people who, doing nothing themselves, believe that nothing can be done,"—at those short-sighted observers who, "associating with industry only the idea of perspiration and fatigue, hail with joy any successful attempts to show that the amount of labor has been overrated."

I shall not contest with you, sir, the palm of pre-eminence in useful efforts to benefit the city or the country. Both of us have labored to the best of our ability, and I trust that neither will suffer unduly from "fatigue or perspiration" on the present occasion. But you have now set me a task requiring effort. You have reared a gigantic, towering structure of statistics, which you call on me to scale—with what success the event will show. For the purpose of over-shadowing the South, you have erected a stupendous pyramid in the North, that all but cleaves the skies. Let us then carefully walk around it,—survey its outline, scrutinize its material, and then compute its contents.

Your address at the Exchange declared that "THE SEAS" were occupied all but exclusively by the North, and that they contributed "$1,400,000,000 annually as their share of commerce in the accumulated industrial product of the people of the United States." To this I answered, that "the seas" produced nothing whatever of commercial value, except the fish caught in them, the annual value of which did not exceed $20,000,000; and that the residue of the $1,400,000,000 carried on the seas consisted wholly of the products of agricultural and manufacturing industry, which commerce had placed on the seas,--in a word, that commerce produced nothing, but only carried commodities which agriculture and manufactures had already produced.

This was so self-evident, that the *Courier* saw the necessity of extricating you from the difficulty, and, accordingly, in its leader of the 8th inst., took you forthwith back to land, stopping just long enough on the sea to glean from it an item of $165,000,000, which that experienced commercial journal ventured to deduce as the commercial profit on our foreign commerce of $560,000,000. Our merchants and shippers will rejoice not a little to perceive that their rate of profit on that amount is fixed at *thirty* per cent. We should pause to say a word as to such a rate on the cotton, specie, &c., forming a part of the $560,000,000, but that there is much larger game ahead. How then did the *Courier* find the residue of your $1,400,000,000 of "commercial product?" It found it by assuming that the labor of carrying and selling a product adds just so much to its value, and must be computed as part of the product itself—that is to say, that the cost of carrying a barrel of flour to market worth seven dollars, being one dollar, the dollar constitutes the commercial portion of the agricultural product.

Proceeding on this principle, the *Courier* then asserted that the total amount of property annually carried by our canals, railways, and coasting vessels, is $5,588,000,000!—that twenty-five per cent. would be "a low estimate!" of the profit produced by transporting this mass of property—and that this 25 per ct. amounted to $1,397,000,000. Such was the process by which the *Courier* demonstrated the truth of your proposition, and exposed what it called "the Quixotism of Mr. Ruggles' sally on Mr. Banks." It was an exceedingly felicitous mode of accomplishing the object,—provided always that the $5,588,000,000 had any real existence, or had ever been transported. I propose therefore to investigate that branch of the subject, and the result will determine which was the Quixotte and which the windmill. I propose to seek this trifling amount of

$5,588,000,000 if I can find it,—to drag it boldly out into broad daylight, to ascertain who owned it, who carried it to market, and what has become of it.

But unluckily for the *Courier*, standing as your endorser, there was one weak spot in its chain of commercial demonstration—and so plainly in sight, that any man or boy who ever saw a canal could detect it—and that was the charge of 25 per cent. for transportation. The idea of two dollars for carrying a barrel of flour, which every canal boatman knows to be carried for less than one,—or fifty dollars for carrying a bale of goods worth but two hundred, was a little too transparent.

It therefore become necessary to relieve the argument from this absurdity, and it could only be done by reducing this rate of 25 per cent. to a more credible figure. But this would require a corresponding augmentation of the amount carried. The adventurous task of duplicating this gigantic amount of $5,588,000,000 was accordingly undertaken by yourself in person, and it forms the central and dominant idea of your letter of the 14th. It is true that you lightened your labor a little, by taking off $200,000,000 from your $1,400,000,000, and assigning it as the share of the fisheries, forests, and mines, thus reducing your commercial product to $1,200,000,000; and therefore it was only necessary for you to stretch the *Courier's* $5,587,000,000 to $9,600,000,000, and by then assuming one-eighth as the profit or commercial product for carrying that $9,600,000,000, your assumption of $1,200,000,000 would come out right.

This tremendous feat you have accomplished. You have ascended the lofty height, and your letter stands sublimely pre-eminent —the Chimborazo of the statistical world. Yes! the Speaker of House of Representatives now stands before the country and the civilized world, proclaiming to mankind that the amount of property annually carried in the United States in their canal boats, railroad cars, ships and coasting vessels is $9,513,512,366 ! ! ! The *Herald* and the *Courier*, in ushering in the astounding intelligence, stamped upon it their respective endorsements—the first declaring that your vindication proved "conclusively that Mr. Ruggles knew very little of the subject he undertook to discuss;" and the second, that "it sustains all we (*Courier*) have advanced in the same behalf, and completely annihilates the figures of S. B. Ruggles, Esq."

And now at the hazard of the "perspiration and fatigue" which the process may involve, I will try to ascend, or, in the vernacular phrase, to "mount" this stupendous fabric of figures. I may venture even to puncture its surface at one or two points, to see how much of it will fade and melt away into thin air.

And in the first place, to throw off all useless weight, I shall substract the $536,000,000 of foreign commerce which you include in the $9,513,000,000, and thus reduce the pile to $8,977,000,000. This modest item of $536,000,000 happens to be a reality, for it is drawn from the governmental official tables, which having no elastic property, are incapable of stretching.

What, then, are the component parts of the remaining $8,977,000,000?

But before proceeding to take it to pieces, let us indulge in one or two general observations. Let us survey the whole, in its general outline, using some known object as a guide in the process of comparison.

In the first place, then, the total assessed value of all the property, real and personal, moveable and immoveable, in the American Union, from the Atlantic to the Pacific, and from the Lakes to the Gulf, is but $7,066,000,000, or less by nearly $2,000,000,000 than the brilliant creation which your magic lamp has called into being and placed in our canal boats, railway cars, and coasting vessels. But such is the power of the sorcery, borrowed, no doubt, from that oriental world with which you so captivated our merchants, that the canal boats, railway cars and coasting vessels of the continent are made to carry a value exceeding, by nearly one third, that of the continent itself.

But, secondly, if these boats and cars and vessels carry nothing but what is actually moveable, then the wonder becomes yet more enormous; for we see, by your own showing, that agriculture produces but $1,600,000,000 and the mechanical arts and manufactures but $1,500,000,000, making an aggregate of $3,100,000,000, and therefore to make up the $8,977,000,000, you must carry to and fro the total product of the country nearly three times over.

But, in the third place, our powers of admiration will reach their utmost capacity, when we deduct from these products the proportions consumed on the spot, and not transported at all by canal boat, car or vessel; and for this purpose let us look a little into some few facts disclosed by our canals. The agricultural product, of all others the most likely to be transported, and thus to enter into internal commerce, is wheat. Of this commodity, 39,000,000 of bushels were produced last year by the five states West of New York surrounding the Lakes, but only 18,000,000 found their way in any shape to the canals of New York. Of the 185,000,000 of bushels of corn in the same district, only 10,000,000 reached Buffalo. Of the 3,126,000 tons of grass produced by that splendid group of grazing states, and returned as "hay" in the census, not one cent's worth entered this state.

And so of the factory and the workshop. Does not every one know how little of the great aggregate of the shoes, the hats, the tin, iron and wooden ware, and the numberless other commodities which a nation uses, is ever carried out of the local districts where they are manufactured? The South, it is true, take largely of some of these industrial products—possibly from the whole of New England $100,000,000 or $150,000,000; but the whole amount of these products transported in other portions of the Union, either by canal boat, car or coasting vessel, does not exceed $200,000,000. The precise amount can be ascertained by an inquiry under the authority of Congress, and I respectfully request your influence to cause it to be made. It must be obvious that it is only *the surplus* of agricultural and mechanical products not needed for home consumption, which ever enters into commerce or is transported on our commercial channels. It is a large estimate to compute that one-third of the total product is surplus, but if it is, it amounts only to one-third of $3,100,000,000, or $1,033,000,000, and that is probably not far from the real amount carried by our canals, railways and coasting vessels.

What then becomes of your fabulous creation of $8,977,000,000? The reality does not exceed $1,000,000,000 or $1,500,000,000 at the utmost, and the residue is nothing but unadulterated moonshine. A celebrated wit declared it to be the office of the political orator "to fill with gas the huge balloon of party." The duty and the best employment of a "fossil" is to furnish the ballast, for bringing the æronaut safely down to earth.

And here I would fain stop, but that you assure me that you have in reserve statistical performances yet more astounding; for have you not filled me with dismay by the declaration, that from "accurate and complete statistical returns we could draw conclusions FAR

MORE SURPRISING than that which has startled" me? Permit me to suggest that the curtain may not rise upon the second act, until we have fairly finished the examination of the first. We have gone but hastily over the general outline of the colossal structure, which you have reared for our especial wonder. Let us now survey it a little more carefully in detail. A thorough criticism of his work is the tribute which the architect most desires.

The vast pyramidal pile now under inspection consists of three grand divisions—the first of railway commerce, value $2,144,000,000; the second of canal commerce, value $1,951,000,000; the third of coasting commerce, value $4,881,000,000—total, $8,977,000,000.

And first of the railways. You assert that they carry an average quantity of 1000 tons per mile, exclusive of coal and iron—that this freight is worth $100 per ton, and consequently that our 21,140 miles of railway carry 21,440,000 tons, worth $2,144,000,000. The arithmetic is very plain, and becomes surprisingly easy when we have no authentic tables awkwardly to check our statistical flights of fancy.

But there happens to be a FACT in your way, and it may come in contact with your airy castle somewhat rudely. The actual returns of railway revenue show that the gross receipts of them all during the year 1855 were but $80,554,000. Of this at least half was for passengers, leaving but $40,277,000 for freight. Now, if you are correct in assuming that the freight of a commodity is one-eighth of its value, then the total value thus transported was but eight times forty millions, or $320,000,000. Your estimate of one-eighth is, however, too large—one-tenth is nearer the truth, and the value carried may have been $400,000,000, but not a cent more. To make this the more certain, I have recently verified the calculation by examining the freights and values on the two great railroads of this state, the Central and the Erie, and I learn from their intelligent officers that their freights are about 6,000,000 of tons, and the values carried about $60,000,000. The value of the whole in the United States being but $400,000,000, the residue of your $2,144,000,000, or $1,744,000,000, melts like mist before the morning sun.

And next of the canals, you assert that they carry on the average 6000 tons per mile—basing your estimate on another assertion, that the New York canals carry 9000 tons per mile. But even that is not true; for the actual amount carried in 1855 on the

877 miles in New York was 4,022,617 tons, or only 4,587 tons per mile.

But who could have imagined that a citizen of Massachusetts, having under his very eyes the sad spectacle of the Middlesex Canal dried up and empty,—the Northampton and New Haven Canal actually occupied as the bed of a railway,—and the Blackstone Canal ruining its proprietors,—could have ventured to claim for them a transportation of 6000 tons per mile, at a valuation of $66 per ton? And yet it is necessary to call into being 600,000 tons, with a value of $40,000,000, and set it all in motion on these defunct old ditches in Massachusetts, to justify the statistical performances of its distinguished representative, and enable him to effect my "annihilation." The total length of the American canals, (including the "Dismal Swamp," and all,) is taken at 4,798 miles. Six thousand tons are then assigned to each mile. Those sums multiplied into each other, yield 28,968,000 tons,—and that multiplied by $66 the ton, brings out into daylight your second born prodigy of $1,951,000,000.

And now for ANOTHER FACT. The canals of New York (excluding from the estimate the coal, which does not exceed twenty millions,) transport more than all the other canals in the United States put together. The value carried by the New York canals in the last year was $204,390,147—to which if you add an equal amount for all the others, you have an aggregate of $408,000,000, instead of your $1,951,000,000, and you are left with a deficit of $1,543,000,000, to follow its misty neighbor of the railway, just put to flight.

And lastly, of the coasting trade, where absurdity has reached its most enormous and preter pluperfect dimensions. I truly regret that there are no authentic tables which enable us to detect, with entire precision, the line between shadow and substance. But it can be discovered, with sufficient certainty, for the present occasion. You assert that 60,000,000 of tons are carried in the coasting vessels, and with solemn accuracy you state the value at $80.60 per ton, making a total of $4,881,000,000!

For the reasons above stated, and guided by the fact that only one-third of our total product goes into commerce, we may take $1,000,000,000 as the utmost possible amount—exclusive of foreign products sent coastwise worth not exceeding $150,000,000. Indeed I am assured, by merchants of experience and intelligence, that even $500,000,000 would be nearer the truth; but I consent to leave you the whole $1,150,000,000, and to send the residue of the $4,881,000,000—being $3,731,000,000—to follow its predecessors out into the fog, making, together, a goodly assemblage of 3,731+1,543+1,744—or $7,018,000,000 of "glittering generalities,"—the whole alike imaginary and delusive. And yet with this empty and shadowy coinage, you have sought to buy the votes of the sober, experienced and sagacious merchants, mechanics and land-owners of this great metropolis—to cure them of their undue appreciation of the importance of the South—to lead them head-long down the dark abyss of national disunion and ruin.

And now, Mr. Banks, let me entreat you, as one of the Representatives not alone of Massachusetts, but of the Union, one and indivisible, to meddle no more with statistics, and least of all in a spirit so partial and disloyal. They are the grand depositories of political, economical and national truth—an element too sacred to be employed, in forging the weapons of the partisan or the fanatic. They are the stateman's eyes, imparting to him a power at once acute and comprehensive—enabling him to scan, with large yet accurate inspection, the whole structure of the state, measuring the noble and giant oak, not only in its deeply rooted trunk and Heaven-piercing branches, but in its minutest fibre and most delicate articulation.

Guided by their clear and tranquil light, he learns to survey, with serene and steady vision, the length and breadth and capacity of a Continental Empire, in all its manifold aspects and necessities—to regulate, with vigorous yet careful hand, its multitudinous yet peaceful movement—to adjust, in finest and loftiest harmony, its vast and varied and seemingly discordant interests. Such is the proper function of the patriot Representative in the American Congress, and such the position that you yourself even yet may fill, if abandoning the poor and petty conflicts of sectional warfare, and rising above the belittling influence of partizan strife, you consecrate your talents, your energy and your future efforts to the preservation of that God-given and precious Union—the best hope of the human race, and the common property and palladium of us all.

With due appreciation,

I remain your fellow citizen,

SAMUEL B. RUGGLES.

NOTE.

Since the publication of the preceding letters, Mr. GUTHRIE, the Secretary of the Treasury of the United States, has presented his Annual Report to Congress, containing a large and valuable body of statistics called for at the last Session.

It embraces, among other kindred matters, the following statement of THE INTERNAL TRADE OF THE UNION, which would seem to settle the principal point in controversy, between Mr. BANKS and Mr. RUGGLES.

A reference to their letters will show that Mr. BANKS, on the one hand, stated the amount at $8,977,000.000 ; while Mr. RUGGLES, on the other, fixed it at less than $1,500,000,000.

The official Report of the Secretary disposes of the question, as follows :

"A reference to the table of production, taken from the census of 1840, will show that our agricultural and manufacturing production in that year amounted to $1,006,133,559; and a reference to the like table of production, taken from the census of 1850, will show the agricultural and manufacturing production, for that year, to have been $2,012,520,539. A like ratio of increase, for the five succeeding years, gives $2,602,363,924 as the value for the year 1855. Suppose $1,000,000,000 to be consumed at the places of production, there is left $1,602,363,924 of production, as the basis of our foreign and internal trade, and the source from which we derive profitable employment for our registered licensed tonnage and our railroads. Take fifteen per cent. of this for our foreign trade, which is about equal to our exports, and there is left

☞$1,352,009,336 for our internal trade,☜

constituting the commercial ligament that binds us together as one nation and one people."

In any further discussion of the commerce of the Union, the $1,352,009,336 thus established by Mr. GUTHRIE, will be assumed as the proper basis of estimate.

NEW YORK, *Dec.* 5, 1856.

www.ingramcontent.com/pod-product-compliance
Lightning Source LLC
LaVergne TN
LVHW011124110826
845150LV00008B/2246

* 9 7 8 1 4 1 8 1 9 5 6 4 9 *